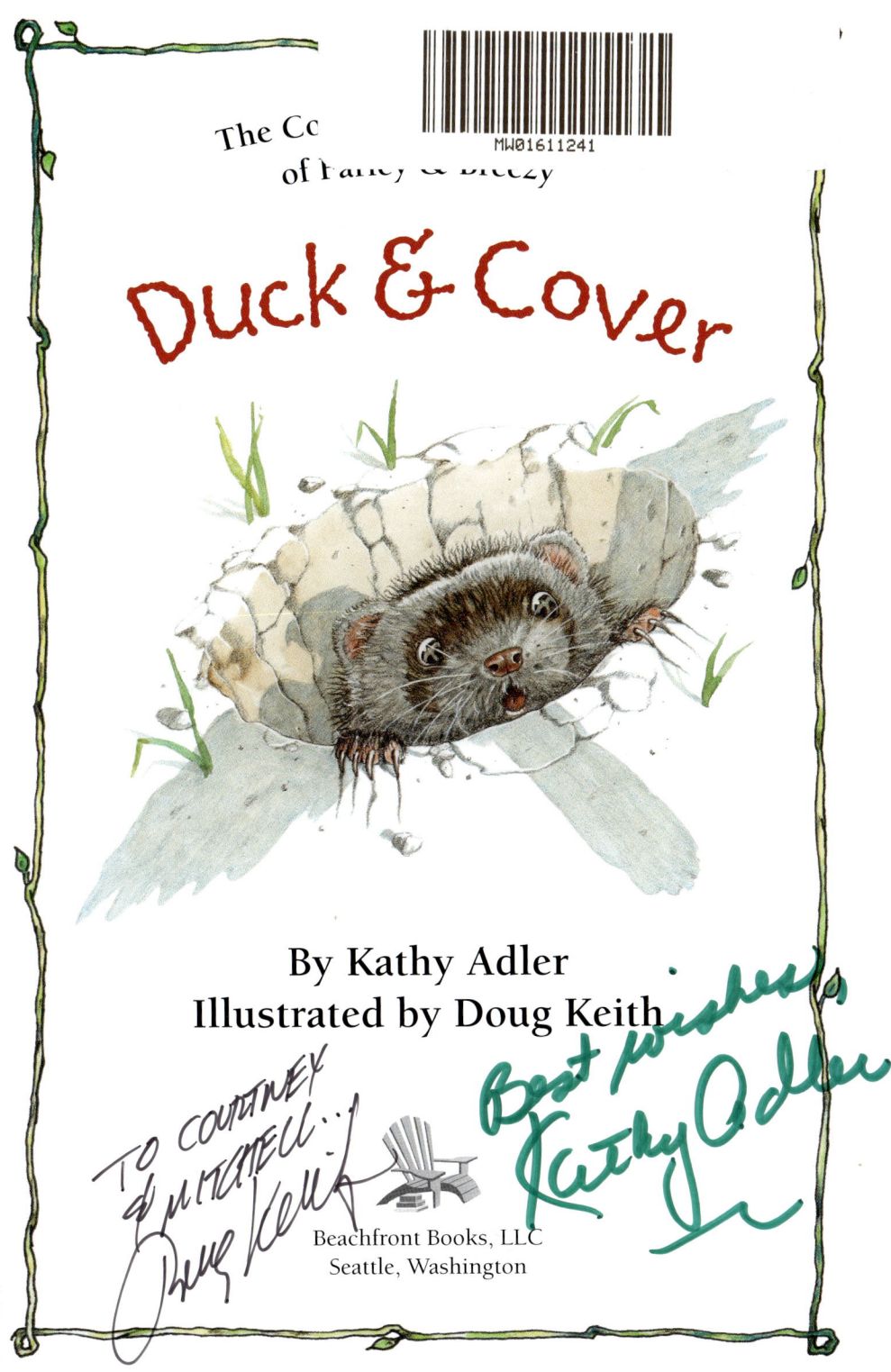

The Co
of Farley & Breezy

Duck & Cover

By Kathy Adler
Illustrated by Doug Keith

TO COURTNEY
& MITCHELL...
Doug Keith

Best wishes
Kathy Adler

Beachfront Books, LLC
Seattle, Washington

To Clare and Donna,
Doug and Molly… our friends.
Farley, Breezy and Kathy

Text © 2006 by Kathy Adler
Illustrations © 2006 by Doug Keith

Library of Congress number 2006931422
ISBN 978-0-9768816-1-2

Published in the United States of America
by Beachfront Books, LLC
Seattle, Washington

Printed in Singapore by Tien Wah Press
Book Design: Molly Murrah, Murrah & Company, Kirkland, WA

Table of Contents

Chapter 1

Babysitters

Aunt Hidey leaves baby cousin Seek with Farley and Breezy.

Farley is asleep under a bush. He awakens when tiny Seek jumps from Aunt Hidey's arms.

Seek races around skreeking and sniffing everywhere.

Breezy sits on a rock in the sunshine and stares at Seek.

Farley's eyes jiggle as he watches Seek race around.

"What do we do with him, Breezy?" asks Farley.

"Aunt Hidey said to play with him," says Breezy.

"He's so little. What do we play?"

Seek throws a stone in the air, does a somersault and catches it.

"I don't know," says Breezy. Maybe he'll get tired and take a nap."

Farley leaps down from his perch. "He doesn't look tired to me."

Breezy stretches. "You know, Farley, it looks like the sun is bleaching out my dark stripe. What do you think?"

Suddenly, Seek goes whizzing by rolling a rock. The rock just misses Breezy.

"Farley. He's heading for the creek," skreeks Breezy.

"Can he swim?"

"I don't know. Run, Farley!"

"Hey, Seek," screeches Farley. "Wait for me."

Chapter 2

Games

Farley runs faster and reaches the riverbank first.

He catches the rolling rock neatly in his mouth.

"Great catch, Farley," squeaks Seek. "Can you do it again?"

Farley drops the rock and rubs his sore mouth.

"Not now, Seek."

"Let's climb that tree over there." Seek scurries over to the tree.

Farley gulps. "Ask Breezy."

Breezy looks at Farley and twitches her long tail.

"Come on Seek. I'll race you to the top," says Breezy.

"I can't go to the top. Mama won't let me."

"How far will she let you go?" asks Farley.

"Right now, only half way."

"Then half way we go." Breezy bounds for the trunk.

Before Farley can sneak away, they're back down the tree.

"That was fun," screeches Seek. "Can we do it again?"

"No. We can't," pants Breezy. "You sit while I catch my breath."

Seek sits.

Farley sniggers at Seek and turns to leave.

"Where are you going, Farley?" says Breezy.

"Uhh... hunting," says Farley. "I thought you'd like a fat mouse."

"Oh, no you don't, Farley. We're in this together."

"Let's go in the creek," shouts Seek. "I'm hot."

Breezy looks from Farley to Seek.

"You go with Farley," says Breezy. "I need a sunbath."

She goes over to a big rock and flops down.

"Can you swim?" asks Farley.

"Of course I can. Mama taught me… but only in the shallow end."

"That's good enough for me," says Farley.

"Last one in has to catch a fish," skreeks Seek. He races off towards the creek.

"Seek. No diving in the shallow end!" shouts Farley, grabbing for Seek's tail.

Chapter 3
Show Off

"Look, Breezy. Farley taught me how to catch a fish."

"Breezy opens one eye and looks at Seek's fish. Her stomach growls with hunger.

"Isn't it the biggest fish you've ever seen, Farley?"

"I think you're right, Seek," says Farley. He drops two more fish next to Seek's.

"Let's eat them now. I'm really hungry," says Seek, tearing apart his fish.

Breezy grabs a fish before Farley can gulp them both down.

"Okay, Seek. It's nap time," says Farley when they finish. "You lie down in the sun next to Breezy."

"No way, Farley." Breezy twitches her whiskers. "We're babysitting together."

"I'm not tired," says Seek jumping and twirling. "Let's all play a game."

"What kind of game do you want to play?" asks Farley.

"Hmmm..." says Seek. "Let me think... I know, hide and seek."

"You might get lost," says Breezy.

"I never get lost." Seek jumps up onto a big boulder.

"I bet you can't find Breezy and me," says Farley.

"Farley. He's too little."

Farley winks at Breezy.

Breezy smiles slyly. "We really know how to hide."

"I can find anyone," says Seek. "I find Mama all the time."

"We'll see," says Farley.

"Do you know how to count to ten?" asks Breezy.

"Sure. No problem," says Seek, swishing his tail.

Seek covers his eyes with his paws and starts to count.

"One, two, three, five, seven…"

Chapter 4

Hiding

"Ready or not, here I come," screeches Seek.

He races from one rock to another looking for Farley and Breezy. Finally, he looks inside an old log.

"One, two, three," he skreeks. "I found Breezy."

"Good for you, Seek," says Breezy. "But can you find Farley?"

"Sure I can." Off he goes again. This time he looks under bushes and behind trees.

Breezy jumps up on a rock and licks off the log bark.

Not far away a hungry hawk glides on the light breeze. She keeps her sharp eyes on the ground below. Seek's quick movements draw Hawk's attention. She drops down for a closer look.

Breezy is about to stretch out for a nap when Hawk's shadow passes over her. She looks up to see large black wings flapping towards her.

"Hawk! Farley! Seek!" she skreeks as she dives from the rock into the underbrush. She looks around for Seek. He sticks his head out from behind a bush.

"Don't move," she hisses.

Seek starts to shake and cry. "I want Mama."

"Hush, Seek," says Farley from a rabbit hole. Slowly he starts to slither out towards Seek. "Stay very still. I'm coming."

Hawk's talons are out and ready as she dives. In the blink of an eye she grabs Seek and pulls him from behind the bush.

"Farley! Help!" skreeks Seek. He wriggles and twists with all his might.

But Seek is too light and Hawk starts to rise.

Hawk has him firmly by the scruff of the neck.

Chapter 5
Finding

Before Hawk can rise, Farley leaps at the bird and clamps onto a wing. Hawk screams as she's pulled back towards the ground.

He holds on with his teeth and front paws and growls.

Breezy shrieks, "Twist harder, Seek. Don't stop."

Hawk flaps her wings. But Farley holds fast. She flaps harder and they all start to rise.

Farley hangs on tight and twists his body around. The heavy load forces Hawk back down towards the ground.

She flies low over some prickly bushes and drags Farley through them. Farley skreeks in pain, but does not let go of Hawk.

Soon Hawk gets tired of the heavy load and drops to the ground again.

Seek escapes.

"I've got him, Farley," says Breezy. She pushes him down a rabbit hole and dives in after him.

Seeing that Seek is safe in the hole, Farley lets go and dives under some prickly bushes.

Hawk is angry. She flies over to the bushes, but they are too thick. She can't reach him.

Finally, with loud screams she flies off.

The woods are silent.

"Farley," Breezy calls softly. "Where are you?"

"Over here," moans Farley. He crawls out from under the bushes.

"Are you okay, cousin Farley?"

"Yes, Seek. I think so. But I'm awfully tired... I need a nap."

"Well, after you rest, can we go hunting? I'm hungry."

Farley and Breezy look at each other and roll their eyes.

"You know, Farley," says Breezy. "Babysitting is not very easy."

"You're right, Breezy. It's harder than catching rabbits."

Chapter 6

Aunt Moana

When the ferrets arrive home, Mama is waiting for them.

"I'm glad you're back," says Mama. "I have to go help Grandma."

"Who's going to stay with us?" asks Farley.

"I thought I'd surprise you. It's your Aunt Moana," says Mama.

"No!" skreek Farley and Breezy.

"What do you mean 'No?' What's wrong with her?"

"She's always moaning about something," says Farley.

"She makes us wait on her," says Breezy.

"You'll be fine and I'll be back soon. Seek, I'll take you home. It's on my way." Mama and Seek scamper off.

"I should have gone with the hawk," grumbles Farley.

"I'd rather roll in dirt and mud," whines Breezy.

Chapter 7
Too Tired Kits

Moments later, a shriek and loud moans are heard coming closer and closer to them.

Aunt Moana shuffles into the clearing. She has mud dripping from her paws and twigs sticking out of her head like tall rabbit ears.

Farley starts to giggle. Breezy slaps his paw.

"Oh. What a frightful trip. I'm a mess," moans Aunt Moana pulling the twigs from her head. She flops down on Breezy's sunning rock. "Come give your Auntie a big hug and kiss, my darlings."

Aunt Moana opens her muddy arms wide.

Farley and Breezy cringe. Finally, Breezy goes over and gives her a dainty kiss.

"Farley, hurry. Your Auntie is so tired she's about to pass out," moans Aunt Moana.

Farley zips over, kisses Aunt Moana and backs away. But Aunt Moana is faster. She wraps her muddy paws around him.

"Oh, Farley. You're soooo cute."

Farley makes choking noises.

"Can I get you something, Aunt Moana?" asks Breezy, hoping her aunt will let Farley go.

Aunt Moana moans, "I'm soooo exhausted." She throws her arms up and places a paw over her eyes.

Farley gulps fresh air. He backs away from her.

"I could use some soft leaves and tall grass, dear. This rock is rather hard."

"I'll get some now." Breezy dashes off.

"Farley, be a good kit and bring me water so I can clean up. Oh, dear. Oh, dear. Just look at me, I'm a mess. Who would have thought coming over a hill and across a clearing would do this to me. Hurry, Farley. I feel faint."

All afternoon the kits are kept running this way and that. With each request, Aunt Moana moans louder and louder.

By early evening Farley and Breezy are *pooped*.

"We have to do something about Aunt Moana," says Breezy. "I'm so tired, my eyelashes are drooping."

"Yeah, Breezy. We have to do something." Farley sits down quietly and lets the wind rustle through his fur. He closes his eyes. Suddenly, he shoots up and looks squarely at Breezy.

"I think I know what we can do," skreeks Farley with a gleam in his eyes.

Chapter 8

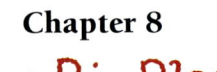 

The Big Plan

Around sunrise, Farley and Breezy are awakened by Aunt Moana's loud snores.

"Whatever your plan is, Farley, count me in," says a sleepy Breezy.

"Well. What if I tell Skunk our aunt has a surprise for him?"

"But Aunt Moana is deathly afraid of skunks."

"That's the whole point," snickers Farley. "When she sees Skunk she'll shriek and scare him into shooting off his scent all over her. She'll never come here again."

"Farley, your plan is perfect," purrs Breezy. "But what can I do?"

"That's easy. You make sure Aunt Moana is standing in the clearing. Then stand behind her so you don't get sprayed."

"Brilliant, Farley. When do we do this?"

"When Aunt Moana wakes up. I'll tell her I'm going to get her breakfast. Skunk likes going out in the morning. He'll be easy to find."

"Ooooo," says Breezy giving him a warm nuzzle. "I can't wait."

With the sun shining through the forest, Farley races to find Skunk. He finds him in a grove of trees.

"Hey, Skunk," calls Farley from behind a tree. He knows that Skunk is very nervous and sometimes shoots his spray first.

Skunk's tail goes up quickly as he looks around. When he sees Farley his tail drops. "Hey, Farley."

"I told my Aunt Moana about you. She said she wants to meet you and give you a surprise."

"What kind of surprise?" asks Skunk twitching his nose.

"Uhhh. Something you'll always remember," says Farley.

"Sounds terrific."

"Yeah," says Farley. "She said to hurry or you'll miss it."

"Oh. I can't wait," says Skunk. "Let's go."

They race through the forest towards the clearing.

Chapter 9

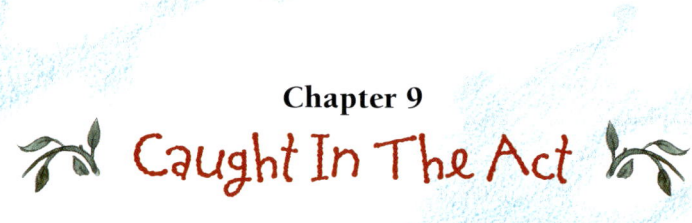

Caught In The Act

While Farley brings Skunk, Breezy talks with Aunt Moana.

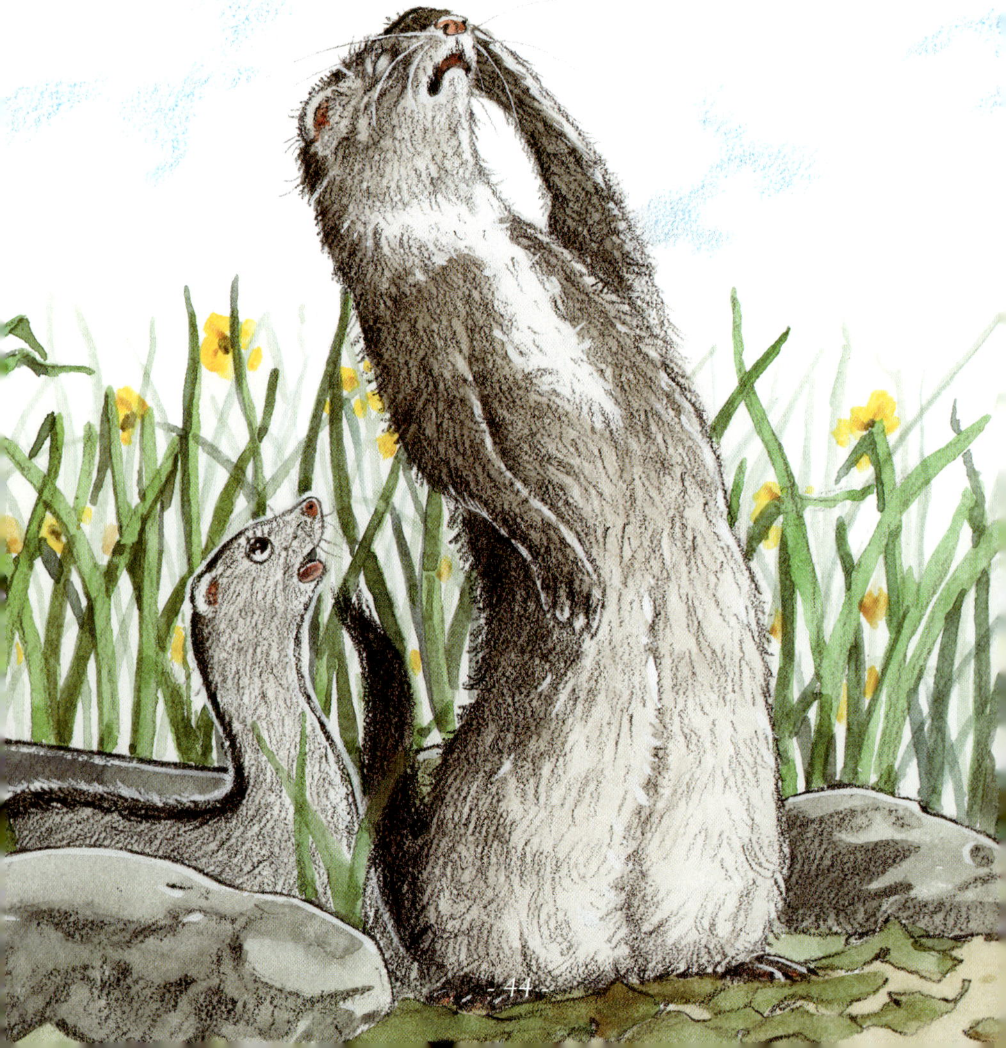

"Breezy darling," sighs Aunt Moana. "I can't go to the clearing. I'm faint with hunger."

"But if you do, you will get breakfast sooner."

"Oh, that is true." She ambles towards the clearing, but suddenly she stops.

"The sunshine there is simply too much for me," she moans.

"But Aunt Moana, the sun will bleach out your tail spots."

Aunt Moana stops moaning and looks at Breezy.

"Do you really think so?"

"Of course," smiles Breezy. "Look how light it made my stripe."

Aunt Moana moves nearer to Breezy. She looks closely at Breezy's stripe. "My goodness. It does look lighter! Hmmm... Being in the clearing would be closer to my breakfast. I could bleach out my spots, too. All right, Breezy. Let's go."

As they come out into the clearing, Breezy sees Farley and Skunk. She looks around quickly to find something to distract Aunt Moana until Farley and Skunk can come closer.

"Aunt Moana," she calls seeing some wild daisies near her. "Look at these flowers. They will look lovely in a daisy chain necklace around your neck."

"Oh, Breezy, you're right," says Aunt Moana. "Let's pick some." She reaches out to pluck the daisies.

"Aunt Moana," says Farley rushing up to her. "I'd like you to meet my friend…"

Aunt Moana looks up. "Skunk!" she shrieks. Her eyes get very wide. Her fur stands up along her back. "Skunk! Skunk! Skunk," she shrieks, even louder.

Skunk shakes. His eyes bulge. He turns around quickly in circles and lets fly skunk spray into the air.

Farley pulls Breezy behind Aunt
Moana. Aunt Moana faints dead
away. She trips Farley and Breezy.
They fall over her and the skunk
spray showers Farley and Breezy.
Skunk takes off running.

Chapter 10

Revenge

Aunt Moana screams. "Get off me, you two. You smell terrible."

Farley and Breezy stand up. Before they can say anything, Mama comes scampering up.

"What is going on here?"

A knowing look comes over Mama's face.

Farley and Breezy look at her then down at their paws.

A moment later, Aunt Moana stands up and throws her arms around Mama loudly crying, "These wonderful kits saved me from a dreadful skunk! They're my heroes."

Mama looks from the kits to Aunt Moana. "Heroes?" she says

"Absolutely!" sobs Aunt Moana.

"We'll talk about that later," says Mama. "In the meantime, I say you *heroes* need a bath."

Farley and Breezy start for the creek. Before they go very far, Aunt Moana calls to them.

"Farley, darling. I never did get my breakfast."

"I'll be glad to get you breakfast, Aunt Moana."

"Oh, Breezy, could you bring me some cool water. I'm feeling faint."

"Of course, Aunt Moana," says Breezy disappearing quickly down the path.

When they reach the creek, Breezy shoves Farley in the water.

"How could you do this to me? I smell like a skunk and now we're stuck with Aunt Moana forever."

Farley does a flip and swims
back towards Breezy.
    "Don't worry, Breezy. I'll think
of something."

🌿 The end. 🌿

Facts From Farley

Since this book is about family, I thought I would share information about my ferret or polecat family. In my ferret family the babies are called kits.

My closest cousins are weasels and minks. Skunks were thought to be cousins, too. Recently scientists said they were not really my cousins even though they have stripes or spots like my ferret family. My weasel cousins look a lot like me. Unlike ferrets and my weasel cousins, minks have long soft fur.

Weasels and ferrets live in the Midwest and eat almost the same things—rabbits, birds, rats and mice. All of my cousins and even skunks like to eat fish. Minks prefer to live near water. They eat water animals such as frogs, crayfish and ducks. Skunks eat mostly plants and sometimes small animals.

All of my family like to hunt at night and sleep during the day. We are brave, except when coyote or bobcat and hawks are around. Remember, a hawk almost got my little cousin, Seek.

Skunks are afraid of owls, hawks, coyotes, bobcats and, of course, my Aunt Moana. If you scare a skunk they'll use their stinky spray on you!

To learn more about my family and cousins visit your school or local library.

Farley's Questions

- Are Farley and Breezy good babysitters?

- Why is Seek only allowed to climb half way up the tree?

- How are Seek and Farley alike?

- Why can Seek only swim in the shallow end of the creek?

- Why is hide and seek a dangerous game?

- Is Aunt Moana fair?

- Does Farley have a good idea for getting rid of Aunt Moana?

- Why does Breezy agree to Farley's plan?

- What would you do if you were skunk?

- Does Aunt Moana *really* believe Farley and Breezy saved her?

- Does Mama *really* believe Farley and Breezy saved Aunt Moana?

About The Author

Kathy Adler loves animals of all kinds, except for snakes. Growing up she had dogs, fish and hamsters. She currently lives with a black lab named Maddie.

Kathy loves to travel. When she visits South Pacific countries, she usually brings gifts of books to the local libraries of those countries. While visiting the Cook Islands in 1997, she met with the librarian there and saw the great need they had for children's books. She has been sending new and gently used children's books there every since. She has also been sending books to a friend in Tonga who shares the books with local children.

Kathy has always loved to write. It was her favorite subject in school. As an adult, she has been writing stories since her children were very young. *Farley & Breezy* is her first published book. She lives in Seattle Washington.

About The Illustrator

Doug Keith's background in commercial art, graphic design and fine art greatly influences his approach to picture book illustration, from story board to finished art. Such versatility earns Doug a wide range of projects, including more than forty illustrated books, a series of popular alphabet posters and numerous fine art commissions.

Among Doug's awards are a television Emmy for graphic design, The Society of Newspaper Design Award for illustration, and *ForeWord* magazine's 2004 Bronze Award for Best Picture Book of the Year, *The Errant Knight*.

Doug's sense of humor and ability to create personality in his characters worked quite well for *Farley & Breezy*. The wacky pair of ferrets can't seem to stay out of trouble and Doug captures this mischievous quality perfectly.

For this project, Doug used water color and colored pencil on illustration board.

Doug lives in north Seattle and commutes daily to his garage studio. To see more of his unique art, visit Doug's Web site: www.dougkeith.biz

Color Me Seek

Color Me Skunk

Color Me Aunt Moana

Don't forget to read the original book, "Farley & Breezy." Farley says he's the fastest ferret. But is he fast enough to catch a juicy rat or a fat rabbit? Read the book and find out...